Purity on Purpose

An Interactive Devotional on Purity

TIFFANY LAVENDER

Copyright © 2016 by Tiffany Lavender
All rights reserved. This book or any portion thereof may not be reproduced or used in any manner whatsoever without the express written permission of the publisher except for the use of brief quotations in a book review.

Limits of Liability and Disclaimer of Warranty

The author and publisher shall not be liable for your misuse of this material. This book is strictly for informational and educational purposes. The purpose of this book is to educate and entertain. The author and/or publisher do not guarantee that anyone following these techniques, suggestions, tips, ideas, or strategies will become successful. The author and/or publisher shall have neither liability nor responsibility to anyone with respect to any loss or damage caused, or alleged to be caused, directly or indirectly by the information contained in this book.

Views expressed in this publication do not necessarily reflect the views of the publisher.

Printed in the United States of America

ISBN:978-0692770863

Keen Vision Publishing, LLC

www.keen-vision.com

For imperfect Christians in His Perfect Will…

Acknowledgements

First and foremost, I give all praise and honor to God. I thank my Heavenly Father for downloading revelation into my spirit for His people. It is such a privilege to be used by God!

God knew exactly what I needed to become the woman of God I am today. I thank Him for my first gift, my family. To my parents, thank you so much for supporting me my entire life. I don't know how I would have made it without your support through every endeavor! I love you guys!

To my sisters, thank you for being such bold examples of Godly women. You two were my first role models, and I thank God for you.

To my friends and ANCC church family, thank you so much for your support. Thank you for creating an environment that pushed me to become the author I never thought I would become.

To my readers, thank you for purchasing this book. Your support means the world to me. I pray that this book ignites the Spirit of God within you!

XOXO,

Tiffany

About the Author

Tiffany Lavender is a native of Tracy, CA and currently resides in Huntsville, AL. She works in the education field by day and is a prayer worrier by night. She is a proud alumni of Jarvis Christian College in Hawkins, Tx and is currently pursuing a Master's degree at Alabama A&M University.

Tiffany is a true servant of the kingdom. She is partnered with All Nations Christian Center, in Huntsville, AL. Under the leadership of Senior Pastor Adrian Davis, she currently serves as the Assistant Director of the Children's Ministry. When asked what drew her to write a book, her response was, "I have known since I was nine-years-old that I would educate people on more than just their 123's and ABC's. This book is one avenue for me to promote spiritual wellness."

Tiffany is the founder of It's a Prayer Thing Ministries. This ministry serves as a prayer request service to those in need of prayer. Over the last two years, this ministry has impacted the lives of people all across the nation, and helped them to understand the importance of prayer.

Contents

Acknowledgements v

Introduction 1

Day One
P.U.R.I.T.Y 3

Day Two
Excuses? Yep, He Died For That Too 5

Day Three
Sight 9

Day Four
I Talk Like This 'Cause I Can Back It Up! 13

Day Five
Hearing 17

Day Six
Let Us Be Great (Pure), America 21

Day Seven
When Purity Meets Testimony 25

Day Eight

Purity in the Weak Moments 29

Day Nine

There You Go Thinking Again 33

Day Ten

Take the Assignment Seriously 37

Day Eleven

Righteousness vs Purity 41

Day Twelve

Change Clothes 45

Day Thirteen

Purity Ain't Fair, but God Is 49

Day Fourteen

Clean Up Your Act 53

Day Fifteen

Pure Relationships 57

Day Sixteen

Sex Zone 61

Day Seventeen

Mix and Mingle 67

Day Eighteen

Is Your Foundation Dry? 71

Day Nineteen

Pair Your Praise with Your Purity 75

Day Twenty

What's the Big Deal? 79

Day Twenty- One

Symbol of Our Love 81

Day Twenty-Two

All Things Through Christ Jesus 83

Day Twenty- Three

Strategic Sharing 87

Day Twenty-Four

Wildest Dream 91

Day Twenty-Five

Double Grace 95

Stay Connected 97

Introduction

Are you ready for twenty-five days of purity? Don't look like that. I already know what you're thinking. Let me break this thing of purity down for you! Purity is defined as being free from contamination and harmful substances. If I bake a cake, I use pure sugar *on purpose*. When I drink water, I drink purified water *on purpose*. For anything I ingest, I intentionally use something that has gone through the process of purification. Living a life of purity requires this same intentionality!

Often times, we get purity mixed up with perfection. *A perfect person doesn't exist, but a pure one does.* Purity is simply the removal of harmful and hazardous substances out of your life. It's time out for picking and choosing which poisons we want to consume, and which poisons we want to flee from. Let's avoid the headaches, heartaches, & life aches and choose to be pure on purpose.

"Dear friends now we are God's children, and it hasn't yet appeared what we will be. We know that when he appears we will be like him because we'll see him as he is. And everyone who has this hope in him purifies himself even as he is pure." 1 John 3: 2-3(CEB)

Just a few things before we move on. At the end of each day are questions about what you've learned. Be sure to answer them honestly. If you make a mistake on this journey to purity, don't give up and throw in the towel on purity. Pray and get back in the ring! Well, if you're ready to begin, flip over to the next page! Let's go!

Day One
P.U.R.I.T.Y

Please **U**nderstand, **R**ighteousness **I**s up **T**o **Y**ou! Anyone and everyone can choose to do the right thing. Why? Because God has granted us freewill to make our own choices. Righteousness doesn't mean perfect, flawless, or errorless, but it also **doesn't** mean reckless, carless or foolish. It means possessing the quality, traits and desire to be Christ-like. Romans 3:22 (NIV) says, "this righteousness has already been given to us." We have all sinned and fallen short, but even with our shortcomings, understand that purity was totally designed for you.

APPLICATION

What is your understanding of purity?

Day Two
Excuses? Yep, He Died For Those Too

When I really don't feel up to doing something difficult, I sometimes convince myself that the task isn't worth my time. I allow myself to come up with every excuse in the book. When I began to notice my lack of personal growth, I realized that this was a horrible habit to have. You see, the devil comes to steal (your task), kill (your dream), and destroy (your purity). The devil desires to keep us complacent in our mistakes. He does this by creating elaborate excuses that seem to be truthful *or at least we keep telling ourselves that they are true*. Jesus died so that we could have life, and life more abundantly. Every sin has already been forgiven. Let me ask you this, what have you done to keep you from living a life of purity?

Oh, yeah. That's right. Absolutely nothing because He died for that too!

APPLICATION

List some excuses that you've told yourself within the last five days.

Now, list five reasons why you CAN be pure!

Day Three
Sight

Purity through vision is significant. Purity through your vison simply means to be conscious of what you watch, look, view, or "study" with your eyes. Protect your sight from anything that is going to breed or produce empty truths. Our vison is another method of digestion. The very thing that we watch rests within us. Sooner or later, we will find ourselves dealing with the same drama as the reality stars, wearing the same clothes as the number one artist, or acting out the same sins from that movie. The Bible says, "The eye is the lamp of the body. If your eyes are healthy, your whole body will be full of light. But if your eyes are unhealthy, your whole body will be full of darkness." (Matthew

26:22-23) To put it simply, we become what we see.

APPLICATION

Write down five habits you have (good or bad). Next to the habit, write someone you know who has the same habit and someone you do this habit with. Finally, write down five people you see often.

My Habits	Who else has this habit?	I usually have this habit when I'm around....

Purity on Purpose   Tiffany Lavender

Five People I See Often...

Day Four

I Talk Like This 'Cause I Can Back It Up!

Being pure through our speech begins with understanding that our words are part of a recipe. What we say (put in the mixture) effects the end results. Be cautious of what you say and who you say it to. Little red riding hood thought she was having a legitimate conversation. No, she didn't curse or speak disrespectfully, but she did entertain a conversation that wasn't pure. Her intentions may have been pure, but remember, it's not impossible for pure people to have impure conversations. She gave out correct information to the wrong person and the conversation immediately became corrupt. The bible says" Let no corrupt talk come out of your mouth"

(Ephesians 4:29 ESV). It also says, "Let there be not filthiness not foolish talk nor crude joking which are out of place but instead let there be thanksgiving." (Ephesians 5:4) As believers striving to use our speech for pure purposes, lets speak with nobility in noble conversations. Yes, that wolf was a smooth talker and the conversation in that moment was harmless, however, the words of the wolf were not backed up by purity. You CAN speak with purity! Why? Because your word can be backed up.

APPLICATION

We have heard the scripture time and time again, "Life and death are in the power of the tongue." (Proverbs 18:21 KJV) Reflect on how you have been using your tongue. What have you been saying? When was the last time you said something encouraging to someone? When was the last time you flipped the conversation once you saw that it was going south? Remember that pure words go a lot further than any other words!

Purity on Purpose   Tiffany Lavender

Day Five

Hearing

We hear everything from our alarm clocks, to our friends, to our jam to our pastor preaching. Our hearing come naturally for most. Believe it or not we hear from God as well. Now will it be a deep Barry White voice that you hear calling on you on the convenience of your cell phone, probably not! John 10:27 says "My sheep hear my voice and I know them, and follow me" (ESV). Be sensitive to the sense of hearing because God doesn't yell. It's one thing to hear the word of God but it's another thing to keep it. Our hearing is a gateway for our purity strategy to be downloaded. If you're listening to foolery, whether it's though music, through conversation or through the devil attempting to plant lies, your purity strategy will be weak. It's very difficult to hear Gods word in one setting then turn around and clash those words with the opposite. Our hearing directly feeds our spirits. No I'm saying don't listen to "worldly music" but I am saying that you have to determine if what your listening to is effecting your purity standards. Does it feed your spirit lies that clash with Gods truths?

APPLICATION

How does what you currently hear daily effect your actions? How will purity effect what you hear?

_____

_____

_____

_____

_____

Purity on Purpose   Tiffany Lavender

Day Six

Let Us Be Great (Pure), America

It blows my mind that even when we try to do good, people attempt to persecute us for our greatness. Jesus dealt with people down playing who he was and what he did. In Matthew 11:16-19, John and Jesus were criticized for doing the right thing. They were at a party and John didn't eat or drink. *He was just chilling.* The party goers accused John of having a demon. Whereas, Jesus was enjoying himself at the party and was accused of over-eating and being drunk (because people CAN'T enjoy themselves unless they're under the influence, right?). In this story, the party goers accused Jesus of everything in the book from being drunk, to being a friend of the tax collectors (the worst people ever), to eventually reaching the all-time high of being a sinner. The irony of it all is that Jesus and John were pure, however, people wanted to place them in the same category they may have been in. Doesn't this sound a lot like the world? People assume that every young person is having sex, going to the club, and living reckless. At the beginning of verse 16, Jesus compares people to children in the market place who can't decide if they want to play happy music or sad music and when they didn't receive the response they desired, they felt like they shouldn't have played either.

Don't allow childish people who don't' know if their going or coming, doing right or doing wrong, living pure or not living pure tell you that you're wrong for doing what God said and what you know is right. They can't argue that purity isn't the way God wants us to live, but people who are frustrated with their lack of greatness will argue that purity is lame and unrealistic. They will attempt to convince you that you're less than because you don't participate in x, y, and z. We have to understand that we are great no matter how society feels about our purity decision.

In 2014, I got my first purity ring. Every time someone asked me about my purity ring, I would get crazy looks, shocking stares, and even laughs. I eventually took my ring off. It wasn't because I wasn't being pure, but because people's reactions to my purity upset me. Now, I wear my purity ring proudly. I don't wear it for people's reactions, but as a symbol of my commitment to God. His reaction is the only reaction I'm concerned about. America may not want you to be great, but God does. There are security and benefits in living a pure lifestyle. It challenges you mentally, but it is well worth it.

APPLICATION

What challenges may occur for you in your purity decision?

Purity on Purpose — Tiffany Lavender

Day Seven

When Purity Meets Testimony

One important component of my purity journey is sharing my testimony. For a long time, I didn't think I had a testimony. I thought that even if I had one, surely no one would be interested in hearing it. It wasn't until I began writing this devotional that God showed me that my purity journey was a very important part of my testimony. Being honest enough to share your triumphs is a form of purity. Hiding behind what or how you wanted your life to be is foolish. Revelations 12:11 says, "And they overcame him by the blood of the lamb and by the word of their testimony, and they did not love their lives to the death." You are already an overcomer because God has already died, forgiven, and healed you from anything you feel is too "bad" or "hurtful" to be in your testimony. You have overcome the lie that if you share your testimony, your purity is out the window. The lie detector test determined that was a lie! The scripture says "Overcome by the WORDS of your testimony" Being all in means trusting God when He tells you to speak. It doesn't matter what people think about your life, you have a purity promise to uphold and you have a testimony to share. Your purity and testimony need a face-to-face. God's already picked the time and the place. You just need to show up.

APPLICATION

Think about every experience that you a have been through. Write down the situations you have experienced that can be used as a testimony.

_____

_____

_____

_____

Purity on Purpose   Tiffany Lavender

Day Eight
Purity in the Weak Moments

SWV has a song that says, "I get so weak at the knees I can hardly speak I lose all control and something takes over me." We all have that area of our purity that can get real tricky. The way our life is set up, we have to train ourselves to not function in that area. Why? Because God hasn't called or asked us to. We have to be honest with ourselves. When we get in the wrong atmosphere, around the wrong person or people, and in the wrong mood our purity can easily be thrown out the window. We get real weak, real quick. It's not a sacrifice if it's easy for you to give up. Yes, purity is a sacrifice. We have to do the opposite of what our human self leads us to do. Living pure in the midst of a world that doesn't recognize a pure life style isn't easy but it's worth it. God's reward for those who choose purity is greater than what we can imagine. If you thought the reward to being impure (living how you want to live) was great in that moment, just imagine what kind of rewards a lifetime of purity brings.

APPLICATION

The key is to living a life of purity is avoiding tempting situations. In order to do this, you must pinpoint your purity weakness. What is your purity weakness? What steps can you make towards not getting caught up in weak moments?

_____

_____

_____

_____

_____

Purity on Purpose   Tiffany Lavender

Day Nine
There You Go Thinking Again

One thought can literally change our lives in a matter of seconds. Our brain is our center. Our brain is where our thoughts are configured. Impure thoughts are real. Often times they get over looked because we can't see them, and they are not displayed where others can see and correct them. This is where discipline plays in. Our thoughts are not for others to correct, they're for us to correct. That's why they're internal. If we are not careful, our thought can have us coo-coo for coco puffs in five seconds. Our natural brains are wired to consistently be in thought. Controlling our thoughts can be harder than controlling anything else. All of our actions begin with a thought. There's an old song that says, "I woke up this morning with my mind, stayed on Jesus." Starting your day with your thoughts in focus is the best advice a song could give. Philippians 4:8 says, "Finally, brothers and sisters, whatever is true, whatever is noble, whatever is right, whatever is pure, whatever is lovely, whatever is admirable if anything is excellent or praiseworthy think about such things." This scripture gives us guidance on where we should focus our thoughts. It's easier to control your thoughts when you know what types of thoughts will yield positive results. Allow this scripture and your thoughts to align.

APPLICATION

What thoughts have you allowed to run crazy in your mind? How will you replace those negative thoughts with positive thoughts?

Purity on Purpose   Tiffany Lavender

Purity on Purpose — Tiffany Lavender

Day Ten
Take the Assignment Seriously

I once had a teacher who was as sweet as pie. I assumed that her kindness meant that the class would be filled with easy assignments and amusement. After we got through the student-teacher introduction, I soon realized that her sweetness was not to be mistaken for weakness. She was not there to give students the opportunity to slack. She took her job very seriously and she expected each student to do the same. When you operate in any of your God given assignments (including being pure because it's an assignment) you have to take it seriously. Don't think that because you have been given grace that you shouldn't take purity seriously. God gave Grace and Mercy as gifts; they are not to be abused. You can't pick and choose when you're going to practice purity. It's all or nothing. Recognize the difference between being a supporter of purity and a doer. It doesn't make sense to support the healthy body initiatives, but never become healthy. Purity is simply a lifestyle covenant between you and God. Why be serious about assignments you don't have to turn in and neglect the ones that actually matter. Take your purity seriously because it was assigned to YOU!

APPLICATION

Create a check list of God given assignments that you would like to get serious about. Remember, no one is expecting you to be perfect. I simply want you to put your thoughts to the paper. Take the first step by acknowledging what you need to work on and know that because of your faithfulness, God will honor you steps.

Purity on Purpose   Tiffany Lavender

Purity on Purpose   Tiffany Lavender

Day Eleven
Righteousness vs Purity

Understand that righteousness and purity go hand in hand. Righteousness is your moral reasoning to do right. Did you catch that? I said to do right, not to do wrong, but to do right. This is what keeps you from being classified as trifling, shady, or fake. The bible refers to righteousness as a law. Today righteousness is and will always be (just in case you thought righteousness was going to fade away) a personal law or purity standard that is mandatory. It's a very simple concept. Children between the ages of one and two understand the difference between right and wrong. Not only do they understand the concept, but they can apply it. So, how old are you again? Okay, moving on. You already have a moral obligation to do right! Purity is following God's rules for your physical and spiritual body. Righteousness and purity go hand-in-hand. Being pure requires you to actually carry out your moral obligation of righteousness. Righteousness sets the tone, and purity is how we follow through.

APPLICATION

List a few ways in which you strive to live in righteousness. Then, list ways you strive to live a life of purity. Once you complete the two lists, review how the two go hand-in-hand. Record your revelation of your life of purity and righteousness!

_____

_____

_____

_____

_____

Day Twelve
Change Clothes

Wardrobes continue to change depending on what's going on around you. You wear clothes according to what is appropriate for the time or occasion. So, what happens when you have made this purity thing official, your spiritual attire is on point, but your physical attire just won't cut it? You switch things up! I am not telling you to go on a shopping spree, but I am saying your clothes should match the new you. You don't do, say, or go where you used to so why should your attire represent those things? Why would you want to wear old habits, old mindsets, and old routines in your new journey? In the work world, they tell you to dress for the job or assignment that you want. What a shame it would be for the boss to want to elevate you, but they can't find you because you're not dressed in the appropriate clothing. Take pride in your outward appearance because inwardly you're pure and beautiful/handsome. With purity comes elevation. With elevation comes glory, but we can't go from glory to glory still wearing flip-flips to business meetings.

APPLICATION

Evaluate your wardrobe. What do you display outwardly? Do you represent purity through your clothes? Do not equate long skirts, long sleeve shirts, alligator shoes, and custom suits to purity. Low cut, revealing clothes, sagging pants, and messy hair don't represent God either. Find your happy medium. Sketch out what that looks like for you. What changes will you make in your attire?

Purity on Purpose

Tiffany Lavender

Purity on Purpose   Tiffany Lavender

Day Thirteen
Purity Ain't Fair, but God Is

On your purity journey, there will be days when you see people living it up and you're going to want a sip of what they have in their cup. There will be days when you want to enjoy life like those who could care less about purity. The reality of this world is that everyone will not choose Christ. Even some of the people who claim Christ won't choose purity. I quickly realized that my purity lifestyle comes with conviction. Sometimes, I feel like it's not fair that I can't get drunk and club like some can without thinking twice about it or feeling convicted. God let me in on a little secret, God never promised that things would be fair. Instead of being angry with those whose spirit doesn't convict them when they don't operate in purity, be understanding. Don't be so quick to banish people to hell because they haven't been practicing purity as long as you have. It's very important to be open and expressive about your purity lifestyle. The same people you are looking through the window at wishing you could take their place for just one day, are the same people looking through your window at your life wishing they could take your place for a lifetime. Share the changes you've made and are making. Share what desires you no longer have and what areas were major struggle areas for you. Like we talked about on Day 7, your purity is a part of your testimony. God wants you to share with others so they can jump on board. Our goal as regular people who happen to be pure is to make the lifestyle look so good that others want to give it a try.

APPLICATION

Write down what the other side of the window looks like for you. Write down some differences between your past and your now.

Purity on Purpose   Tiffany Lavender

Day Fourteen
Clean Up Your Act

When cleaning your purity room (your life), there may be some old things you have to throw away, put in place, fold up and hang up. When I was little, my room always managed to get dirty. It never failed. As soon as my room was out of control I knew my mom and sisters were going to tell me to clean it. I didn't want my dad to have to say anything about my room, because if my father had to step in I knew I would be in trouble. When I wanted to give the appearance that my room was without cleaning it, I would stuff everything under the bed. Not realizing that my mom was smarter and would check under the bed. Her response was, " If you clean I right the first time and maintain your room throughout the week (clean little by little), you wouldn't have to worry about your room getting overwhelmingly dirty. She was right. This principle also applies to my spiritual purity room as well. Do a deep clean. Put every emotion, issue, distraction and accomplishment where it belongs. Pick up the standards you dropped on the floor. Organize the scriptures you've learned, so that you can find them when you need them. The goal here is to actually get rid of the mess, not to hide it.

APPLICATION

Write down seven things that need to be cleaned in your physical house. Now parallel those seven things to seven things you can do to maintain your purity.

Example: *Bathroom: The bathroom is where you release waste from your body, and cleanse yourself of the day. You may need to release people or things that waste your time and take up space.*

Purity on Purpose   Tiffany Lavender

Purity on Purpose

Tiffany Lavender

Day Fifteen
Pure Relationships

The word relationship doesn't just define romantic connections. It defines your connection with your family, friends, co-workers and/or church members. I simply just want to give some words to the wise. That means you will receive these words if you're wise. James 3:17 says, "But the wisdom that comes above leads us to be pure, friendly, gentle, sensible, kind, helpful, genuine and sincere." (CEV) Being in a pure relationship is possible and obtainable. The Bible says in Amos 3:3, "How can two walk together unless they agree?" Everyone in the relationship need to be in agreement with their roles and expectations. Let's stop using the excuse "They love God because they go to church!"

Remember I'm referring to all relationships. Going to church is great and loving God is even better, but if someone hasn't decided that they want to live their life for God and according to His purpose for their life, then love doesn't mean a thing because they are lacking a relationship with Him. Church doesn't prove or justify a relationship, neither do the word "Christian". We have to pay attention to a person's lifestyle and life decisions. If you have never discussed with your best friend, boyfriend, girlfriend, wife, husband, family, etc. that you desire for all of your relationships to have a common denominator (God and purity), then you cannot hold anyone to a standard that you have never expressed. Purity does not mean perfection. Every relationship won't be picture perfect, but your relationships should not produce gossip, lies, pain, hurt, sin, dysfunction, or stupidity. Take heed of people who are not striving towards the same purity goals as you. God's image (his wisdom, love, kindness and peace) should reflect from the top to the bottom and between every crack of your relationships. Allow your prayer to be that all of your relationships will become pure alliances chasing virtue.

APPLICATION

List three people you have a relationship with. Examine how and why those relationships were started. Do you think you have been consistent in each relationship? Does each person know the status of your relationship with God? Take some time this week to talk to these people about your life choices and how you plan on staying pure on purpose.

Purity on Purpose

Tiffany Lavender

Day Sixteen
Sex Zone

From the title, you have figured out what Day Sixteen will be about. I decided that this portion of this wonderful devotion would be genuine. We will not tip-toe around the truth because God doesn't tip-toe around the truth. Here are the facts about the sex zone:

ABSTINENCE

Abstinence is abstaining from sex until you're married. The Bible says in 1 Thessalonians 4:3-4, that the will of God is that we maintain sexual immortally and control our bodies. Immorality means corrupt or sinful. In other words, out of pocket. It's out of pocket for you to be having sex unmarried. Simple. Nowadays, there is a term called "bases". This approach attempts to justify sexual immorality by moving from first base, to second base, to third base and sliding into home at fourth base in a time frame. My advice is to not play the base game. It doesn't matter how long you've been with someone, or how much they profess to love you. Having sex unmarried is a sin, and should be avoided. Wait for God to send your home run moment. Don't try to create one.

MASTURBATION

This action is done for self-gratification. The key word is self. It's a selfish act. If God wanted you to please yourself, there would be no need for the opposite sex. Both men and women have sexual needs. God designed for these needs to never be felt until after you're married. It's not until we start unlocking the mysteries of sex before its time that we deal with the issue of our "needs" not being met. Controlling those needs is the key. What you need to do is fulfil God's needs first (your purity) and your personal needs will be taken care of. Philippians 4:19 says, that God will supply all of your needs according to His riches in glory. If God will supply all of your needs, why are you trying to fulfill them yourself? Masturbation opens the door for the devil to use sex to rule you, and no one has time for that.

Sex is not a taboo topic that should never be discussed. It's actually a God-given gift meant to be enjoyed. The issue is that people can't control their desire to wait on their gift. One of the spiritual gifts is self-control. Your self-control today will make your gift that much more brilliant.

MYTH

Once you're married you don't have to practice purity anymore!

That's a lie. Your purity should continue until you die. Remember, sex is only a sin if you are unmarried. Purity doesn't only mean abstaining from sex until marriage. You must also practice purity in your marriage. For instance, people have made it okay to bring other men or women in their marriage bed to "spice things up." There is no such thing as spicing up your marriage by bring other people into your marriage. This is impure. A marriage is one man and one woman. Adultery doesn't have a place in your marriage. The bible say that the marriage bed is to be undefiled.

Remember, Purity isn't just about abstinence. Abstinence is great, but that's only a portion of purity. Don't get so focused on not having sex that you forget God has also called you to love, tell the truth, be positive, respectful, faithful, and obedient. Sin is sin no matter how you dress it up. Remove yourself from temptation and allow your purity to win.

APPLICATION

Write down some myths you've heard about purity. Research the word of God and apply the Truth to those myths.

Purity on Purpose — Tiffany Lavender

Purity on Purpose Tiffany Lavender

Day Seventeen

Mix and Mingle

Meeting people can be a hard task for some and easy for others. The concept of mixing and mingling simply means to integrate yourself into an atmosphere of diverse people. Mixing and mingling gives you the opportunity to meet new people, discuss views, and talk about real life. Hebrews 10:25 says, "Not forsaking the assembling of ourselves together, as the manner of some is; but exhorting one another: and so much the more, as you see the day approaching." (KJV). Don't get in the habit of shying away from believers. It's great to experience people from all walks of life, but don't get so caught up in trying to teach the nonbelievers that you only surround yourself with nonbelievers. At some point, you will need some like-minded people to pour back into you. So the big question is, how do you meet these like-minded people? How do you meet people who have chosen to live pure on purpose? I have asked myself that question a million times. They definitely don't just knock on your door. You have to go out, mix, and mingle. Go to events, open up your mouth and talk to new people! Get connected to organizations and ministries you find interesting. Host gatherings and invite a friend of a friend. I decided to write a devotional because I believe that this devotional will be an opportunity to get connected to people who are trying to concur purity day-by-day like myself.

APPLICATION

When was the last time you put on your best to mix and mingle? I love getting dressed up. I used to get so hyped to get ready for the club! Why? Because it was an opportunity to feel good, look good, and enjoy myself. We should be able to have that same excitement in any atmosphere. I still get just as hyped to go to social events. I didn't change my preparation, just the location. How much effort, energy, and time did you spend on things that didn't glorify God? How can you put that same effort, energy, and time into your purity life style?

Purity on Purpose   Tiffany Lavender

Day Eighteen
Is Your Foundation Dry?

Wow! We have been discussing purity for eighteen days! I pray that you have gotten some clarity on purity and its importance. Purity is a gradual thing. Each level of accomplishment is meant to be built upon. What you learn at the beginning stages are needed to understand and function at the next stage. When you make the decision to be pure, you learn how to see yourself in a whole new light. You realize that a lot of the decisions you make affects everyone around you. You become a living example of how God designed all humans to be. Identifying your process takes time. You must allow each level to dry before you pour on a new layer. Allow your purity foundation be poured and settled before you try to move on. If you try to build on a foundation that isn't dry yet, your building won't stand. Master your self-worth, let your purity goals sink in, and allow your pure lifestyle to become solid. Then, you can move on to putting up your frames. Purity is absolutely a process, but it doesn't mean you live a lifetime with an undried foundation. At some point, your foundation should start to solidify. Don't be the one who is looking at everyone's mansion as you sit on an empty lot with all the materials you need to build. You have the same potential to have a mansion! If you haven't decided that you want to be pure (with your actions, heart and lifestyle), you haven't began to work on your foundation. If you haven't established what and how to operate in the basic requests of God, your foundation isn't dry. It's a God and you thing. The more you release to God, the quicker your foundation solidifies.

APPLICATION

Take some time and create a prayer. Focus on receiving clear instruction on what should be built on your purity foundation. Ask God what he specifically wants you to accomplish through your purity.

Purity on Purpose   Tiffany Lavender

Day Nineteen

Pair Your Praise with Your Purity

Praising God is one of the most honorable gifts you can give God. The Bible says, "He inhabits the praise of his people." Meaning he dwells where the praise is. Let's connect the dots. If praise is an honorable gift that we can give God and purity is an honorable gift we can give, what would happen if we put the two together? You will create an unstoppable combination that man nor can the devil break! You have just hit the double Jeopardy. Your purity covers the promise and your praise secures it. Your purity is the guideline for every promise, gift, and blessing God designed for you. Your praise is the guide that secures all of those wonderful things safe from the gates of heaven to your door step. If we pair our praise and purity together and God dwells in the mist of your praise, doesn't that mean God dwells in the midst of your purity as well? God understands every nook and cranny of your purity because He's in the midst of it with you. Do you think God would challenge you with purity then leave you without guidance or assistance? No, God will be right there watching, aiding, teaching, and mending. You will defiantly have a reason to praise if you pair it with your purity.

APPLICATION

Today, take 5 minutes to praise God for keeping you from the danger that was meant for you, but couldn't find you. Keep in mind that what your purity does is cloak you/consume you so that multiple dangers fly right past you! When you live a life of purity, you are covered in God's righteousness.

Purity on Purpose   Tiffany Lavender

Purity on Purpose   Tiffany Lavender

Day Twenty
What's the Big Deal?

At the end of the day, what's the big deal about purity? As followers of Christ, we eventually get to a point where our desire is to align with God's vision for our life. We should go from experiencing life to the fullest without God to experiencing a full life with God. Contrary to the myths, living a life of purity allows us to live freely. You don't have to worry about contracting a STI/STD or sharing awkward after sex moments with someone you barely know. You don't have to deal with soul ties that bind your emotions to someone's emotions your emotions were never meant to be bound to. You don't have to experience mental wars due to false realities you have created. The big deal is that purity is not fictional; it's a biography, a description of our real life. Purity has never been the trending topic, but it's always trending on God's Lifebook page. Purity is not something that we should take for granted. It's right up there with world peace and expanding God's kingdom. It's that important! True love is found through purity; peace is found through purity. If you want to make God smile, make your purity a big deal.

APPLICATION

Let's make some steps toward making purity be trending topic. Create a hashtag and put it on all of your social media outlets. Make people want to know what #purityonpurpose is!! If you don't have social media, strike up a conversation about Purity on Purpose with a friend, family member, or church member.

Day Twenty-One
Symbol of Our Love

The number one question was on the board. It read, "Name one object that can be worn, that symbolizes love?" A ring was the number one answer. Previously, I discussed wearing a purity ring. A symbol of your promise to God should be taken seriously because it's an outward expression of our love for God. We have to get to a point where we love God so much that we are willing to display our purity externally. Wearing a purity ring, bracelet, t-shirt or what every your symbol is won't make you pure, but it does open the door for you to share your purity journey with others. Your struggle and triumphs may be the encouragement or conviction someone may need to break the stereotype of a person living in purity. Have you ever thought about the fact that God loves you so much that he purposely designed a lifestyle meant to protect and secure every promise and blessing created for you? He thought enough of you to protect you from the disasters that could be avoided. If we don't thank God for anything else, let's thank Him for the gift of purity. (Even if you haven't opened your gift yet, it does negate the fact that you have the gift!) Choose a symbol of love that represents your purity. Walk boldly with your symbol of purity. Don't let anyone shame you for enjoying your present.

APPLICATION

We all love gifts. Gifts are not required, they're voluntary. God's gift to us is the gift of purity. Return the favor by wearing a purity symbol at minimal. I challenge you to figure out what your purity symbol will be and wear it with pride.

Take a picture and tag @purityonpurpose on your social media. We would love to see your symbol of love!

Day Twenty-Two
All Things Through Christ Jesus

I've been asked a multitude of questions when it comes to my purity. Is it hard to abstain from sex? How did you made the decision to be pure? I tell them that there are harder things in life than no having sex. The only way to be successful in your purity is to fully dedicate your life to Christ. Purity is a hard concept for some to grasp, especially someone who has not dedicated their life to Jesus Christ. Your salvation allows your mind to be renewed. You literally become a new person. You tackle life completely different. You find fulfillment in working unto God. You don't stop being human, but life is put into perspective for you. Purity becomes you. We can do all things through Christ Jesus. Purity doesn't work without having our own personal relationship with God. Strategy on how you need to operate through your purity journey comes from your communication with God. I know that the only reason I've been able to endure this life of purity is because of God's grace and mercy.

APPLICATION

Years from now, when you're telling your children and grandchildren about your legacy, what details of your purity will you include? Write below a prayer for guidance and strategy for your purity journey.

_____

_____

_____

_____

_____

Purity on Purpose
Tiffany Lavender

Day Twenty-Three
Strategic Sharing

Prayerfully, this devotional is helping you understand what purity is and how to easily implement purity into your life routines. I pray that you're excited and intrigued by this thing called purity. As you learn more about living a life of purity, open our mouth and share the gift of purity with others. You don't have to preach a ten-page purity sermon. You can simply share something that you learned or a revelation God has revealed to you. Be a magnet. God loves when we talk about things that are pleasing to Him. If God provides you a chance to speak about righteousness, self-control, kindness, temptation or any other topic related to God, you need to speak. You would be surprised at how God can turn hearts in a conversation. You will find yourself being the source of encouraging words and wisdom. God has called us to be the light. It makes no sense for us to be a light hiding under a bowl. Allow your purity journey to shine and draw others into the movement.

APPLICATION

How will you strategically share purity with others?

_____
_____
_____
_____
_____
_____
_____
_____
_____

Purity on Purpose   Tiffany Lavender

Purity on Purpose

Tiffany Lavender

Day Twenty-Four
Wildest Dream

Never in my wildest dreams would I have imagined that my life would have taken the course that it has. Through it all even through every change, I never stopped dreaming. I figured out the God's ream for me has always been to incorporate my purity with His dream for me. Thank the lord God never stopped dreaming for us. Even when our dreams didn't match his and when we tried to walk in someone else's dream for our life. I believed that our wildest dream isn't dreamed by us but by God. Gods plans for us are so legitimate that we don't even have to worry our heads with handing the dream. We just get to live it. Being pure on purpose isn't a fantasy, it happens every day in today's world.

Purity = Wildest Dreams= Your Destiny

APPLICATION

Compare and contrast your dreams from 10 years ago to now.

_____
_____
_____
_____
_____
_____
_____
_____

Purity on Purpose

Tiffany Lavender

Purity on Purpose

Tiffany Lavender

Day Twenty-Five
Double Grace

Twenty-Five. The number of double grace. You ending to start a new beginning. If you haven't learned anything else, you have learned that purity brings new blessings that would have never been unlocked otherwise. God's grace provides you with safety and protection. Who couldn't use double protection and safety, especially from ourselves? We cause issues for ourselves but luckily, God's grace is not contingent upon our behavior. In the story of Job, God doubled his animals and inventory. Don't miss out on your scoop of double grace. Allow your inventory to be doubled just like Job because of your faithfulness to your purity. Be pure on purpose so God's grace can double, triple, and overflow over the rest and the best of your life.

Stay Connected

Thank you for purchasing Purity on Purpose! Tiffany wants to stay connected with you! Below are a few ways you can reach out to Tiffany. For more information about Tiffany or It's A Prayer Thing, visit www.itsaprayerthing.org.

We look forward to hearing from you!

INSTAGRAM Tiffany Lavender

FACEBOOK Tiffany Lavender

PERISCOPE tiffany_lavender

Made in the USA
Las Vegas, NV
15 November 2021